NATURE UNDERCOVER

Published in the United States in 2000
by Blackbirch Press, Inc.
260 Amity Road
Woodbridge, CT 06525
web site: http://www.blackbirch.com
e-mail: staff@blackbirch.com

Copyright © 2000 by McRae Books Srl, Florence (Italy)
First Edition

Growing Up was created and produced by
McRae Books Srl, via de' Rustici, 5 – Florence (Italy)
e-mail: mcrae@tin.it

Text: Beatrice McLeod
Illustrations: Antonella Pastorelli, Paola Holguin, Andrea Ricciardi di Gaudesi, Ivan Stalio, Matteo Chesi
Picture research: Anne McRae
Graphic Design: Marco Nardi
Layout and cutouts: Adriano Nardi and Ornella Fassio
Color separations: Litocolor, Florence

Printed in China

10 9 8 7 6 5 4 3 2 1

Library of Congress Cataloging-in-Publication Data
McLeod, Beatrice.
    Growing up / by Beatrice McLeod.
        p. cm.
    Includes index.
    ISBN 1-56711-501-2 (hardcover : alk. paper)
    1. Animals—Juvenile literature. 2. Reproduction—Juvenile literature. 3. Growth—Juvenile literature. 4. Animal behavior—Juvenile literature. [1. Animals—Infancy. 2. Growth.] I. Title.
QL49 .M5188 2000
590—dc21
                                                                                99–009436

NATURE UNDERCOVER

Growing Up

Beatrice McLeod

Illustrations by Antonella Pastorelli, Paola Holguin, Ivan Stalio

Series Consultant:
Jim Kenagy, Professor of Zoology and Curator of Mammals,
Burke Museum of Natural History and Culture, University of Washington

BLACKBIRCH PRESS, INC.
WOODBRIDGE, CONNECTICUT

Contents

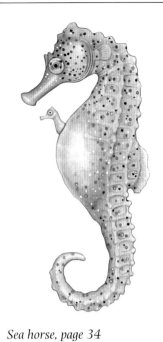

Sea horse, page 34

Silkworm, page 27

Elephant, page 31

Barn owl, page 22

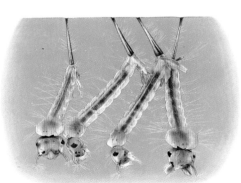

Mosquito larvae, page 26

Night monkeys, page 34

Introduction

For most animals, producing young, caring for them, and successfully raising them, requires a great deal of time and energy. Mammals, in particular, expend a great deal of effort to raise their offspring. This is because mammal young are often completely helpless at birth. Many other animals, however,—insects and other invertebrates, for example—are self sufficient from the moment they enter the world. In this book, we will see how all kinds of animals are produced, and how they feed, grow, learn, and survive during the early part of their lives.

Crocodile, page 14

How this book works

Getting Fed
PREDIGESTED "FISH SOUP"
Pelican chicks have huge appetites. Their parents have to work hard to supply them with food during the first weeks of their chicks' lives. Pelicans are strong, skillful fliers that sometimes travel hundreds of miles each day to find food for their young. Male and female parents offer a special pre-digested and regurgitated "fish soup," which their offspring dig out of their parents' bills.

Each chapter in this book begins with a stunning, two-page illustration that shows young animals as they are born or hatched, and as they grow. These openers lead into double-page spreads with many illustrations, showing a variety of youngsters as they go about their lives, learning the skills they will need to survive as adults.

Brief captions explain how each spot illustration relates to the subject.

Vivid, descriptive text accompanies a large illustration that provides a stunning, up-close view of nature in action.

Detailed illustrations highlight specific adaptations.

A dynamic, full-color illustration introduces each section subject.

The introductory text gives an overview of the subject.

Getting Fed

Young animals need plenty of nutritious food and water to help them grow. Many species of insects and invertebrates—such as earthworms—are able to feed themselves from birth. Among other animal groups, particularly birds and mammals, one or both of the parents feed the young until they are old enough to hunt or find food for themselves.

Preparing for Young

A LONG, COLD WINTER. Emperor penguins breed on the South Pole's freezing Antarctic ice. In autumn, they leave the Arctic waters and head inland for several miles. There, they pair up and mate. By May, the female produces a single large egg. Her partner takes the egg onto his feet and covers it with the skin of his abdomen. The female, having spent a good deal of energy producing the egg, returns to the sea for food. Then, the Antarctic winter sets in. For two whole months the males, often as many as 25,000 of them in one rookery (breeding colony), huddle together waiting for spring to arrive. When spring comes, the eggs hatch, and their partners return.

Birds' eggs, tucked inside their carefully prepared nests, come in many different colors. Some species lay brightly colored eggs, while others lay dark or speckled eggs that blend into their surroundings.

Preparing for Young

For most animals, reproduction is the key event of their lives. Some choose a partner weeks or even months ahead of time. Finding or preparing a safe place to lay eggs or to give birth can also take a while. Some animals, like the Pacific salmon, make long journeys to spawning grounds far from where they spend most of their adult lives. Most birds build nests specifically for the purpose of laying their eggs and then protecting them. Once a bird mother's young can fly, the nest is most often abandoned. With most animal species, much of the preparation for reproduction is done by the female, but some fathers take part in family care.

Many snails, including the **Roman snail** shown here, lay their eggs in shallow holes in soft, damp soil. Then, they cover the eggs with more soil to keep them safe from predators. Tiny, baby snails, only .3 of an inch (9mm) long, emerge after 20–30 days.

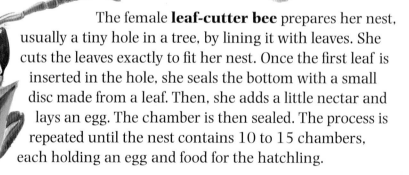

The female **leaf-cutter bee** prepares her nest, usually a tiny hole in a tree, by lining it with leaves. She cuts the leaves exactly to fit her nest. Once the first leaf is inserted in the hole, she seals the bottom with a small disc made from a leaf. Then, she adds a little nectar and lays an egg. The chamber is then sealed. The process is repeated until the nest contains 10 to 15 chambers, each holding an egg and food for the hatchling.

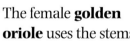

The female **golden oriole** uses the stems and leaves of plants, wool, and even paper, to fashion her nest. She begins with the stems, carefully weaving them around horizontal twigs to form the framework. When her nest is finished, she lays her eggs inside. Both parents help feed the young.

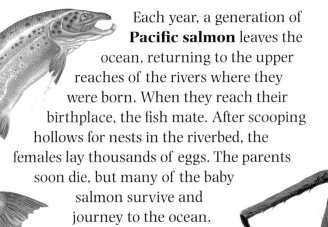

Each year, a generation of **Pacific salmon** leaves the ocean, returning to the upper reaches of the rivers where they were born. When they reach their birthplace, the fish mate. After scooping hollows for nests in the riverbed, the females lay thousands of eggs. The parents soon die, but many of the baby salmon survive and journey to the ocean.

For safety, the female **hornbill** seals herself inside her nest, leaving just a small hole through which her partner gives her food. She stays inside until her chicks are half-grown.

The female **nursery spider** carries her eggs in a ball of silk attached to her fangs. Normally a fast, agile hunter, she becomes so weighed down by her load that she stops eating. When the eggs are ready to hatch, she cuts a hole in the silken egg sac so that her spiderlings can scramble out.

The female **conch** lays up to 2,000 egg capsules, each containing hundreds of eggs. Inside each capsule, the first 10–30 eggs that hatch feed on the other eggs. They eat the eggs until they grow large enough to emerge from the capsule.

During autumn, the female **Orgya recens butterfly** lays her eggs on the undersides of the leaves of rose and thorn bushes. There, they are hidden from view until spring, when they hatch.

The male Australian **mallee fowl** spends months each year constructing an incubator for his partner's eggs. First, he digs a hole that he fills with grass and leaves. Then he covers it with sandy soil, leaving a special chamber where the female lays her eggs. When the female is done, the male seals the mound. As the vegetation inside decays, it produces heat that helps to incubate the eggs.

Life Begins

BREAKING OUT! Like most reptiles, leopard tortoises hatch from eggs. The female deposits her eggs in a sandy, sheltered spot, where they will be safe and warm until they hatch. The baby tortoises develop inside their leathery shells for several months. Then, using a special "egg tooth" on their jaws, the hatchlings pierce the shells. First, their heads appear. Then, gradually, with the help of their front legs, they struggle out of their shells, into the sand, and begin their life out in the world!

Life Begins

Some animals wait only hours or days for their young to be born. Others wait for weeks, months, or even years to see their offspring. Some young are more developed than others. Most mammal babies are born fully formed. Many marsupials, however, are born only partially developed. Bird young—and many amphibian and reptile young—hatch from eggs. Most insects lay eggs inside which larvae form. After the larvae hatch, they undergo major changes before reaching adulthood.

All **crocodiles** lay hard-shelled eggs. The females bury them in shallow holes or mounds near the water, above flood level. Many crocodile mothers guard their nests for 2–3 months until the eggs hatch.

Most insects lay eggs in which larvae develop until hatching. This **caterpillar** (which is a butterfly larva) is hatching from its oval-shaped egg where it has survived by getting nutrients from liquid yolk. Some caterpillars bite their way out of their eggs; others simply grow until they burst out.

1

Bird eggs are nearly perfect packages. They contain high-quality nourishment for a chick as it develops inside. The shells are porous, which means the oxygen a chick needs to breathe can enter and the carbon dioxide it expires can get out. Eggs are just hard enough to provide protection to a developing bird. But they are also sufficiently fragile, so a tiny chick can peck its way out when the right time comes. This sequence of illustrations shows a chick as it breaks out of its egg and struggles to its feet for the first time.

2

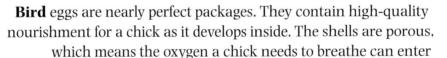

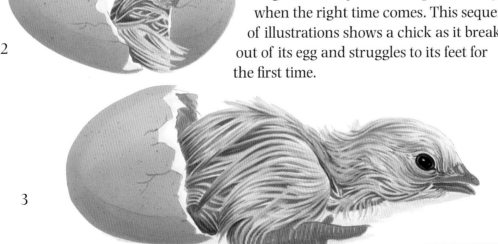

4

3

Most **snake** mothers lay eggs. They choose a damp, secluded place, lay their eggs, and then cover them with sand or soil. Then they leave. Only a few species, like this viper, stay with the eggs until the snakelets hatch.

Aardvarks live in the southern half of Africa. The females give birth to one baby, usually during the rainy season. With its long, tubular snout and its hairless, wrinkly body, a newborn aardvark is a strange-looking mammal!

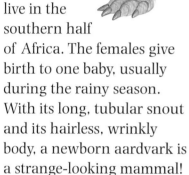

Most frogs produce eggs that hatch into long-tailed tadpoles and then develop into adults. **South American rainfrogs**, however, hatch from their clear, jellylike eggs looking like fully formed little froglets.

Like most young herbivores of the African grasslands, **zebra** foals are on their feet just 20 minutes or so after birth. They need to be able to run soon after birth to avoid being eaten by predators.

Female **elephants** live together in groups. While one of them gives birth, one or two other females keep her company. They stroke the mother-to-be with their trunks. They also help the baby to its feet once it is born.

Baby **kangaroos**, called joeys, weigh only a small fraction of an ounce (less than 1 g) when they are born. Blind and naked, they crawl into their mother's pouch and hook their mouths onto a teat to drink milk. They do not leave the pouch permanently until they are almost a year old.

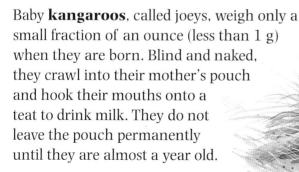

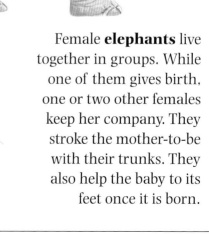

The Fight for Life
YOUNG EATING YOUNG. The female of one species of ichneumon wasp uses a clever device to ensure that her larvae will have plenty of food when they hatch. Using her very sensitive antennae, she locates the larvae of wood wasps beneath the bark of trees. Then she uses her long ovipositor (tube for depositing eggs) to bore into the wood and deposit her eggs in or next to the larvae. When the ichneumon eggs hatch, they feed on the wood wasp larvae. When their host is consumed, the ichneumon larvae spin cocoons in which they develop into adults.

Female **leopards** have short gestation (pregnancy) periods. They give birth to their cubs just 3 months after mating. Immature at birth, the cubs are very vulnerable. A mother leopard keeps her young hidden in a den, but if she thinks a predator knows their whereabouts, she will move her family to a new hiding place. The cubs stay with her for the first 18 months of their lives.

This three-month-old **spider monkey** is chewing on a tough jungle leaf as it learns how to feed. It will need very sharp teeth as an adult to feed on the tough plants and stalks of its jungle habitat.

The Fight for Life

Some animals can take care of themselves from the moment they are born. They know by instinct how to maximize their chances for survival. Many insect, reptile, amphibian, and fish young, for example, never even see their parents. When these creatures are hatched or born, they are already on their own. Many mammal young, however, require months or even years of learning, feeding, and protection from watchful parents.

Staying close to a parent is often the best way to keep safe. This baby **frog** is riding on its parent's head.

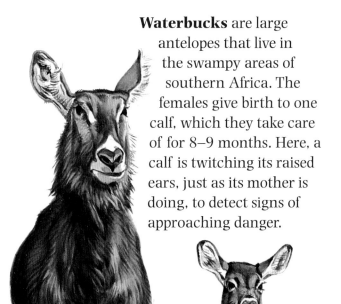

Waterbucks are large antelopes that live in the swampy areas of southern Africa. The females give birth to one calf, which they take care of for 8–9 months. Here, a calf is twitching its raised ears, just as its mother is doing, to detect signs of approaching danger.

The **blue-footed booby** lays two eggs, but within a day or two of hatching, one of the chicks kills the other. Although this seems cruel, it ensures that the remaining chick will get all the food and attention it needs to reach adulthood.

Female **cuckoos** do not build their own nests. Instead, they lays eggs in the nests of other bird species. When the cuckoo egg hatches, the much larger cuckoo chick will push the host's eggs out of the nest. This way, the cuckoo receives the undivided attention of its "foster parents."

Golden eagles, and many other birds of prey, often lay two eggs at different times.This strategy increases the chances of successful breeding. If something happens to the first chick, a second, younger chick may still have a chance.

Leatherback sea turtles lay their eggs on sandy tropical beaches. When the eggs finally hatch, the tiny turtles face a perilous journey across the sand to the sea. Seabirds and crabs attack the babies as they scuttle across the beach.Once near the ocean, predatory fish wait for them in the waves.

In early spring a female **snowy owl** scrapes a hollow in the ground and lays her eggs. Within just a few days of hatching, the chicks are covered in a thick, warm coat of feathers, called down. The mother covers her owlets with her body to protect them from the freezing Arctic winds.

Getting Fed
PREDIGESTED "FISH SOUP"
Pelican chicks have huge
appetites. Their parents have to
work hard to supply them with
food during the first weeks of
their chicks' lives. Pelicans are
strong, skillful fliers that
sometimes travel hundreds of
miles each day to find food for
their young. Male and female
parents offer a special predigested and regurgitated "fish
soup," which their offspring dig
out of their parents' bills.

Barn owls are well liked by farmers because they feed on the mice and rats that are pests in fields and barns. The owl shown here has caught a sparrow, which it is taking back to its nest to feed its young.

The **shoebill** or **whale-headed stork** lives in the marshlands of central Africa. It has a large beak for scooping up the fish, amphibians, and other animals on which it feeds. But its beak is also used during the hot African summer to carry water to chicks in its nest. As the chicks grow, they learn to drink the water their parents bring them 4 or 5 times each day.

Getting Fed

Young animals need plenty of nutritious food and water to help them grow. Many species of insects and invertebrates—such as earthworms—are able to feed themselves from birth. Among other animal groups, particularly birds and mammals, one or both of the parents feed the young until they are old enough to hunt or find food for themselves.

Like all mammals, this **field mouse** mother suckles her offspring. As they grow, they will begin to eat the buds, seeds, and nuts that their mother brings to their underground den. Soon afterward, they will learn to find their own food.

Partially developed **earthworms** are deposited in the soil 24 hours after their parents mate. After 2–4 weeks, the tiny worms emerge fully formed and able to fend for themselves. They reach maturity at about 90 days after birth.

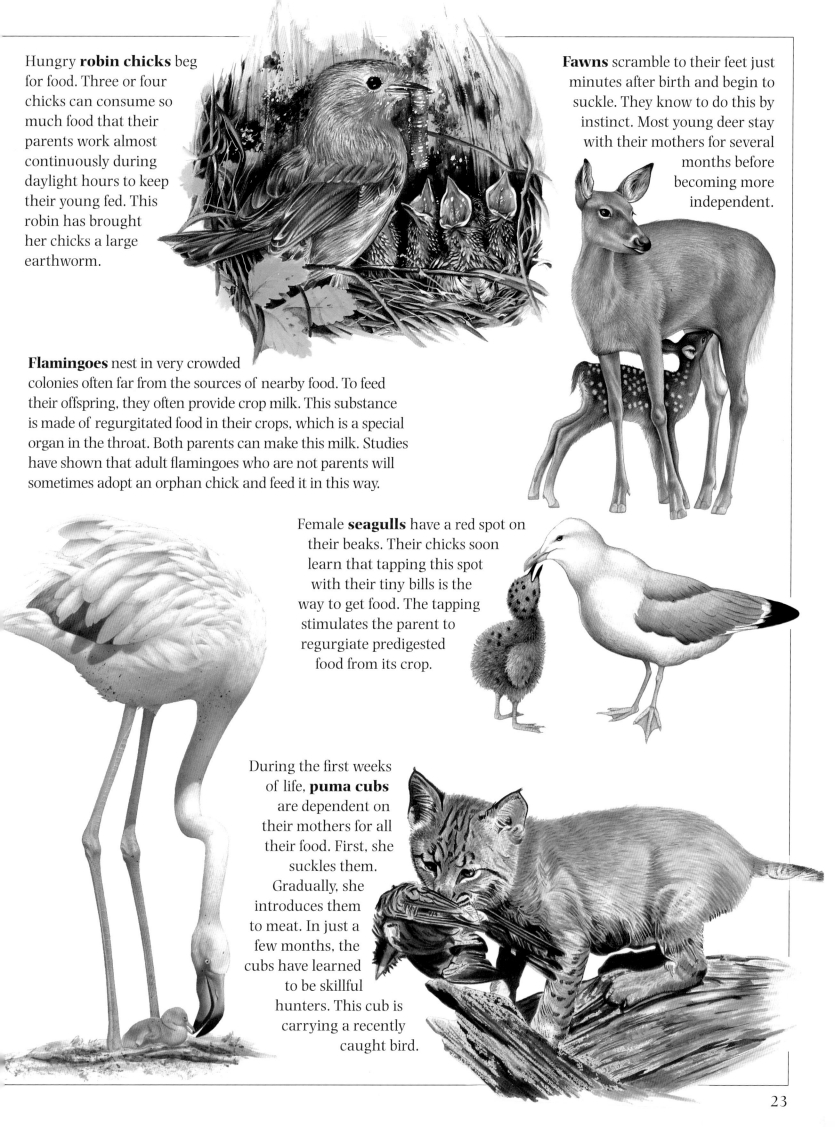

Hungry **robin chicks** beg for food. Three or four chicks can consume so much food that their parents work almost continuously during daylight hours to keep their young fed. This robin has brought her chicks a large earthworm.

Flamingoes nest in very crowded colonies often far from the sources of nearby food. To feed their offspring, they often provide crop milk. This substance is made of regurgitated food in their crops, which is a special organ in the throat. Both parents can make this milk. Studies have shown that adult flamingoes who are not parents will sometimes adopt an orphan chick and feed it in this way.

Female **seagulls** have a red spot on their beaks. Their chicks soon learn that tapping this spot with their tiny bills is the way to get food. The tapping stimulates the parent to regurgiate predigested food from its crop.

Fawns scramble to their feet just minutes after birth and begin to suckle. They know to do this by instinct. Most young deer stay with their mothers for several months before becoming more independent.

During the first weeks of life, **puma cubs** are dependent on their mothers for all their food. First, she suckles them. Gradually, she introduces them to meat. In just a few months, the cubs have learned to be skillful hunters. This cub is carrying a recently caught bird.

Stages of Life

COMPLETE PHYSICAL CHANGE. Most frogs undergo three major stages of life. They start out as eggs, laid in the water or in damp places on land. The eggs hatch into little round-bodied tadpoles with long tails. Tadpoles live in water and breathe through their gills. This stage lasts from a few days to up to 3 years, depending on the species. Near the end of the tadpole stage, lungs and legs begin to develop, and the tail disappears. The adult frog is amphibious, which means it can live in water or on land.

Stages of Life

Most animals pass through a series of life stages on their journey from birth to old age. Many of the most striking changes occur in youth. Some animals, like frogs or butterflies, undergo very distinctive physical changes. Others, like pumas or manatees, maintain the same basic body shape they were born with. They just become larger, stronger, and more agile as they grow.

Adult **golden eagles** have beautiful feathers and long, strong wings. This chick will have to wait for 4 years before it develops into a large, majestic, adult bird of prey.

For the first few weeks of their lives, **penguin chicks** are covered in thick, warm feathers, called down. This is gradually replaced by their distinctive black-and-white feathers.

4. Adult butterfly.

3. Pupa (chrysalis).

A striking physical change in appearance from one life stage to another is called "metamorphosis." Insects undergo some of the most dramatic metamorphoses. The illustrations here show the **swallowtail butterfly**'s 4 life stages. The adult female lays eggs on the leaves of a flower or tree. These eggs hatch into caterpillars which, in turn, become pupae (chrysalises). After a few weeks, the adult butterfly emerges from the pupa and sets off to feed and look for a mate.

2. Caterpillar (larva).

Common **mosquito larvae** hang upside down under the surface of the water using their long syphons to breathe. The larvae pass through a pupa stage before developing into adults and leaving the water for good.

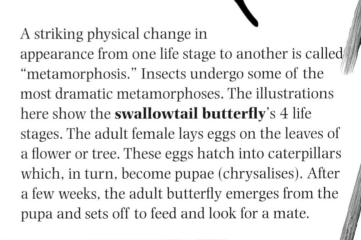

1. Butterfly eggs.

The striking plumage of the adult **scarlet ibis** is highly visible in the mangrove swamps and forests of Central America, Mexico, and the southern United States where this bird lives. The chicks are not as bright—they have two-toned brown-and-white feathers until they become mature.

This **silkworm** caterpillar is looking for a place to spin its silken chrysalis. Silk farmers harvest an average of 2,625 feet (800 m) of silk from each chrysalis, but it takes 50,000 chrysalises to make 2.2 pounds (1 kg) of raw silk.

These **cricket nymphs** already look like miniature versions of their parents. They will soon turn into full-grown adults.

Manatees, also known as **sea cows**, are aquatic mammals of the rivers and coasts of the Caribbean, the Amazon, and West Africa. A single, tiny calf is born to a female every second year. The calves are born fully formed—they even have their premolars and molars (teeth).

This **puma cub** (also known as a **cougar** or **mountain lion**), like most mammals, will keep the same body shape for its whole life. Its ears and paws are proportionally larger than they will be in adulthood.

During its second larval stage, the **Atlantic lobster** is still only .4 of an inch (10 mm) long. Before reaching adulthood, the larvae go through several stages during which they change their outer shell.

Learning

PLAY FIGHTS AND MISCHIEF. Up to five or six red fox cubs are born in each litter. During their first few weeks of life, the helpless cubs lie quietly in their den. But as they grow, they become more adventurous, seeking out fun and mischief. One of their favorite pastimes is fighting and wrestling among themselves. Although this may seem to us like it's just for fun, it is actually a key learning experience. As they wrestle, the cubs strengthen muscles, hone reflexes and coordination, and learn to judge speed and distance—all essential skills for hunting.

Learning

Many young animals have a lot to learn before they can survive by themselves. Baby birds, for example, need to figure out how to fly. Both bird and mammal babies have to learn how to find food for themselves, and how to avoid becoming food for someone else. The young learn these general skills either on their own by trial and error, or they are taught by their parents.

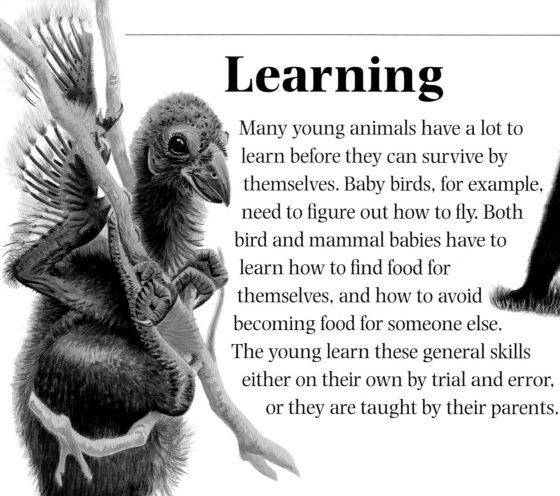

All growing mammals love to play. These **grizzly bear cubs** are battling it out in a mock fight. Like the foxes on the previous pages, play fighting helps them develop strength and coordination.

Hoatzins inhabit the northern rain forests of South America. This nestling is just beginning to explore the idea of flight, but it still has a lot to learn before taking to the air.

Although adult **otters** are perfectly at home in the water, youngsters—who are born in dens on land—have to be taught to swim. They begin swimming lessons at about 8 weeks.

Hedgehogs feed on a variety of foods, including earthworms, beetles, slugs, caterpillars, birds' eggs, carrion, fruit, nuts, and seeds. When they are big enough, hedgehog young go on foraging trips with their mothers. They soon learn what is good to eat and what should be avoided.

Raccoons forage at night near streams and marshes. There, they feed on frogs, fish, and crayfish that they hook out of the water with their front paws. They also eat birds' eggs, insects, and fruit. They sometimes get food from garbage cans in urban areas.

The big step for almost all baby birds is learning to fly. This **hummingbird** nestling is perched on the edge of its nest, ready to go.

Elephants live in hot climates in India and Africa. To stay cool, they roll in muddy rivers and spray themselves with refreshing river water. This survival skill is learned from an early age.

All birds use their beaks for cleaning and maintaining their feathers—called preening. Water birds, like this **duckling**, spread an oily substance over their feathers to help keep them waterproof.

De Brazza's monkeys live in swampy forests in central Africa. During the first few weeks of their lives, the young monkeys cling to their mother's fur. Then they learn to swing quickly through the treetops by themselves.

Red squirrels are born in holes in tree trunks. They leave their nest for the first time at about 45 days and soon learn to become nimble climbers. They are fully independent at about 8 weeks.

Mother birds, like this **seagull**, teach their chicks to recognize and make calls that will help them communicate with her and other birds. Studies have shown that some chicks react to their parents' calls even before they hatch.

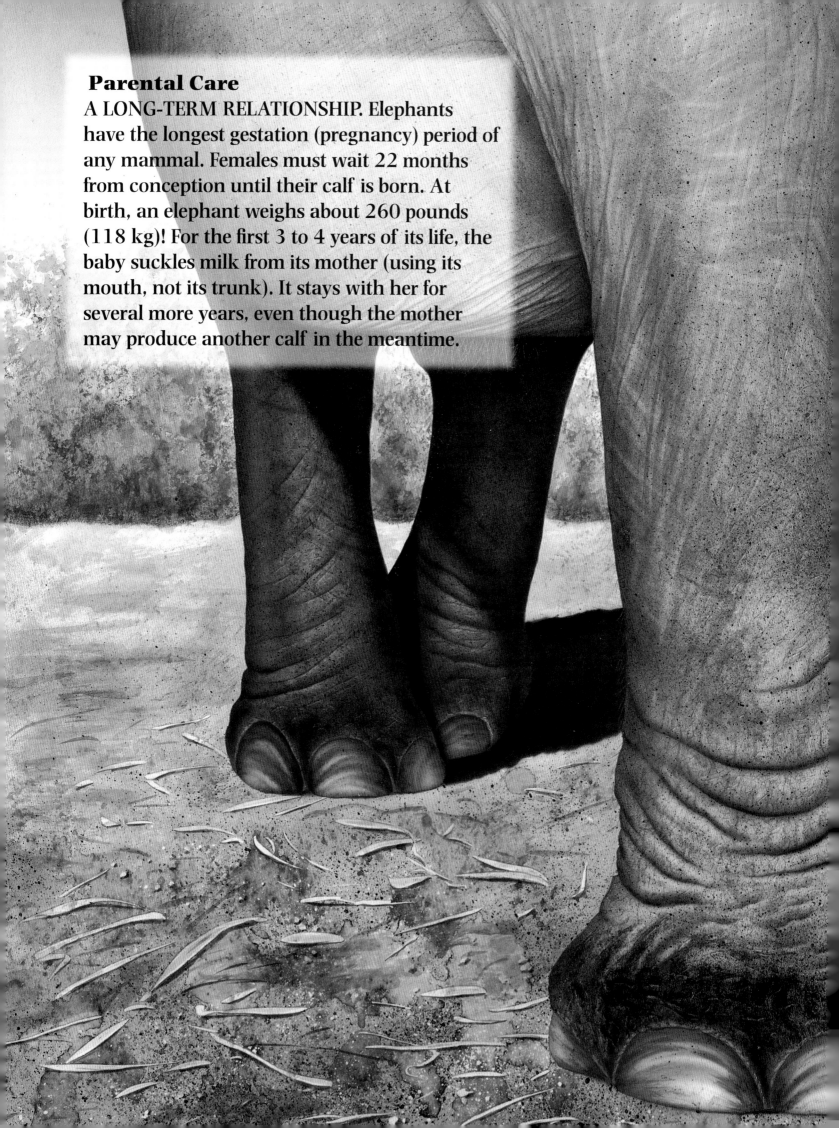

Parental Care

A LONG-TERM RELATIONSHIP. Elephants have the longest gestation (pregnancy) period of any mammal. Females must wait 22 months from conception until their calf is born. At birth, an elephant weighs about 260 pounds (118 kg)! For the first 3 to 4 years of its life, the baby suckles milk from its mother (using its mouth, not its trunk). It stays with her for several more years, even though the mother may produce another calf in the meantime.

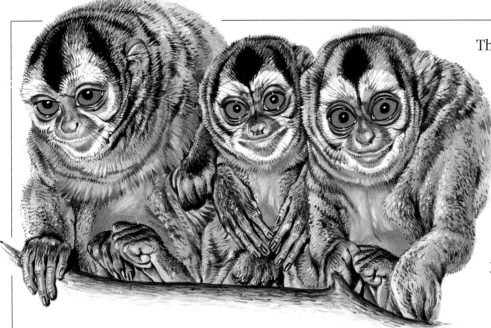

The **night monkey** is a nocturnal inhabitant of the Amazon rain forest. Female night monkeys give birth to 1 baby every year, but each baby stays with her for 2 years. This means mother night monkeys are usually caring for two youngsters at a time.

Male **sea horses** actually "give birth" to babies. They have a special pouch on their stomachs into which the female lays her eggs. The male then fertilizes the thousands of eggs and keeps them safe in his pouch until they are ready to hatch.

Parental Care

Some mothers abandon their eggs as soon as they are laid. Many animals that provide little parental care will lay a huge number of eggs so that, even without parental help, the chances are good that some young will survive to adulthood. Where only a few eggs are laid, or a small number of babies are produced, parents take a more active role in protecting and raising the young. The female parent often does the care, but in some cases, fathers also lend a hand.

Chimpanzee mothers give birth to 1 baby after 8–9 weeks of gestation and nurse their young for 2 or 3 years. During that time, they form a very close bond, which continues even after the chimp becomes an adult.

This baby **owl** is peering out from inside its safe cactus den. Its mother laid her eggs in an old woodpecker nest, which is an ideal home for baby owls. Here, they are shaded from the searing desert heat, and the prickly thorns of the cactus discourages predators.

Newborn **scorpions** crawl up onto their mother's back, where they are safe from predators. They stay on her back for up to 6 weeks. During that time, they absorb water through her skin and feed on reserves built up before birth.

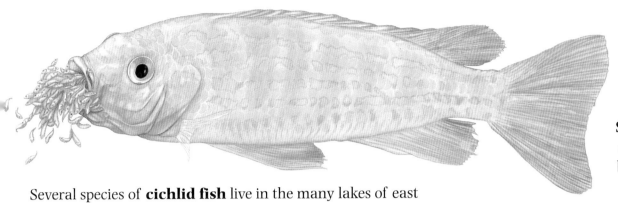

Several species of **cichlid fish** live in the many lakes of east Africa. To keep her eggs safe before hatching, the mother fish keeps them in her mouth. To make sure she doesn't swallow the eggs, she doesn't eat anything during the entire 10 days before they hatch. During the first week of their lives, the young race back to their mother's mouth when danger threatens.

Sloths do not make dens or nests. When they give birth to their single baby, the youngster hangs onto its mother's long fur for the first 6 months of its life.

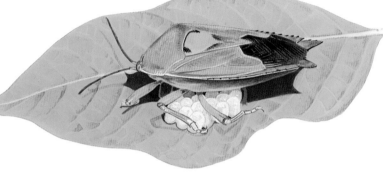

Very few insects take care of their eggs or young, but female **shield bugs** are one of the exceptions. They defend their eggs from predators and parasites by shielding them with their bodies.

The Australian **duck-billed platypus** is one of the world's most unusual mammals—it lays eggs instead of giving birth to live young! The only other mammals that do this are echnidas (spiny anteaters). Once the eggs hatch, the mother platypus protects her young from predators and suckles them just like other mammal mothers.

Families

Animal families generally stay together only while the offspring require their parents to feed, train, and protect them. As soon as the young are able to care for themselves, the family dissolves. When new babies arrive, a new family is formed. Some animals, however,—lions and elephants, for example—live together in longlasting groups that include many members of the same family. Female elephants and lionesses even help other group members care for their young. A mother may leave her baby in the care of a sister, aunt, or grandmother.

Koalas live in eucalyptus trees in eastern Australia. A female gives birth to 1 baby that lives in her pouch for about 7 months. The baby clings to its mother's fur until it becomes independent, at around 11 months.

Wallabies are small Australian kangaroos. Like their larger cousins, they give birth to an immature joey that bonds with its mother while inside her pouch.

Pronghorn females give birth to 1 or 2 fawns after 8–9 months gestation. Although the fawns can run faster than a human being just 2 days after birth, they are still not fast enough to avoid predators. For the first few weeks of their lives, their mothers keep them hidden in long grass. The fawns stay with their mothers until they are about 5 months old.

White storks nest in western Europe during the spring and summer. The female lays between 3 and 5 eggs that, when hatched, are fed regurgitated insects and fish. The chicks all leave the nest at about 18 weeks of age.

Grizzly bears mate in spring, but the female delays the development of the fertilized eggs until fall when she enters her winter den. She gives birth to 2 or 3 very small cubs (about 12 oz/340 g), which she looks after for anywhere between 2 to 4 years.

Fox kits are born in burrows that are either dug by the vixen (female) or borrowed from other animals. Born in the spring, they stay with their mothers—learning how to hunt—until the end of summer.

The massive **rhinoceros** of Africa and Asia gives birth to a single calf, which weighs about 140 pounds (64 kg). The calf will most often stay with its mother until the birth of the next calf, which usually occurs after about 2 to 4 years.

Mother **bantams** hatch their brood after sitting on the eggs for several weeks. The chicks are soon able to take care of themselves.

Female **elephants** live together in herds led by an older female, called the "matriarch." She heads a group that is usually made up of her sisters, daughters, and female cousins, all of whom will help one another with care of the herd's young.

Lionesses live together in prides led by one or several dominant males. Females produce litters of 2 or 3 throughout the year and help one another raise their cubs. Some females will even suckle cubs other than their own.

For More Information

Books

Bailey, Jill. *How Caterpillars Turn into Butterflies* (Nature's Mysteries). Tarrytown, NY: Marshall Cavendish Corp, 1998.

Crewe, Sabrina. *The Kangaroo* (Life Cycles). Chatham, NJ: Raintree Steck-Vaughn Publishers, 1997.

Merrick, Patrick. *Earthworms* (Naturebooks). Chanhassen, MN: Childs World, 1999.

Walker, Sally M. *Manatees* (Nature Watch). Minneapolis, MN: Carolrhoda Books, Inc., 1999.

Web Sites

Enchanted Learning

www.enchantedlearning.com

Find out information on butterflies, frogs, bears, and other animals at this kid-friendly site. Features printouts of hundreds of animals.

San Diego Zoo

www.sandiegozoo.org

Learn about and see photos of the animals at the San Diego Zoo.

Index